A Silent Fight

The strength behind the struggle

A Silent Fight

The strength behind the struggle

RACHEL HARRIS-WALKER

Text Rachel Harris-Walker
Copyright © Rachel Harris-Walker

First print March 2025

To my dad, my hero.
You were my greatest supporter, my best friend, and the one who showed me what unconditional love really is. Through every moment of my life, your unwavering love and encouragement were my anchor. I can never put into words just how much you meant to me or how deep our bond was, but this book is my attempt to honor you and the profound impact you had on my life.
Losing you has left me with a broken heart, but your love gives me the strength to keep going. I miss you every day, and I'll carry your memory with me always.
This book is for you, Dad, with all my love, forever and always, 100% Daddy's girl.

CONTENTS

CHAPTER 1: "DADDY'S BABY GIRL" — 9

CHAPTER 2: LIFE ON STANTON STREET — 17

CHAPTER 3: LOVE FOR A LIFETIME — 27

CHAPTER 4: BUILDING OUR FAMILY — 35

CHAPTER 5: DREAMS TAKING FLIGHT — 47

CHAPTER 6: CREATING THE GOOD LIFE — 53

CHAPTER 7: THE WILL TO FIGHT — 59

CHAPTER 8. LOSING DADDY — 65

CHAPTER 9. FIGHTING THE DARKNESS — 73

CHAPTER 10. FINDING THE LIGHT — 83

CHAPTER 11. REACH FOR THE SUNSHINE — 93

ACKNOWLEDGEMENTS — 103

ABOUT THE AUTHOR — 107

CHAPTER 1: "DADDY'S BABY GIRL"

While playing outside with friends, I would see my daddy coming down the street. I felt so happy to see him that I would start running home. He always got out of his car with open arms, waiting for my embrace. He was so strong and loving! He never raised his voice at me, because I was his baby girl. My friends and my siblings' friends used to run with us to meet him because they knew he would have popsicles for us to hand out to our playmates. — Rachel's journal

◊◊◊

As a child growing up in Detroit in the 1970s, I felt carefree. The air seemed cleaner back then, and to this day, the smell of fresh air takes me right back to Stanton Street where my daddy worked hard to give my mother, my siblings, and me a good life in a house of our own. As a jitney, Daddy drove a car all day, taking people home with their groceries from a local store called Farmer Jack's.

My parents hadn't always lived in Detroit. They grew up in Camden, Arkansas, and came north looking for better opportunities in life. My daddy, Leandro Frank Harris, was born in 1938 and grew up in a household with six siblings. His father was a stern man who demanded a lot of respect. I can

A SILENT FIGHT

remember visiting Arkansas at age 15 and seeing my father remove his hat when he walked into the house, addressing my grandfather with "Yes sir," and "No sir."

Daddy only told me bits and pieces about his childhood, mainly that he had to leave school after the eighth grade to pick cotton and cut down trees to help support the family. One of his brothers was adopted, and he lost a sister in a house fire. He married my mother, Girtha Lee McKenzie, and although they started their family in Camden, they had three more children in Detroit, with me being the last born.

Upon coming north in 1964, my parents were taken in by Daddy's older sister Mary who had already moved to Detroit along with their sister Sarah. My aunt Mary provided housing for my family and helped with bills and food until Daddy got on his feet.

My father worked for Castle Steel at first, providing a good living for Mama, my two brothers, four sisters, and me, but an injury forced him to go on disability. He could have lived solely on disability payments, but Daddy was a hard worker and didn't like to sit at home, doing nothing. That's when he began working as a jitney. I came along in 1971 when Daddy was 32 years old. Daddy spoiled me rotten, and he always introduced me to everyone as his "baby girl." I had a bottle until I was about five years old! Daddy encouraged my older brothers and sisters to treat me special too, since I was the baby of the family.

Mama didn't like me being spoiled. Whenever Daddy wasn't around, she made sure I knew I was just another one of her children and she refused to give me special treatment.

A SILENT FIGHT

To family and friends, my nickname was "Shelly." Everybody called me that, but my mother never addressed me by my name. She always said to others, "This is my last one, and I'm not having any more." While my father was affectionate and affirming of me, my mother felt that I was spoiled enough and she wasn't going to add to it. I don't remember her rocking me or holding me in her arms like my dad did.

Daddy's skin was a light vanilla color; he was strong, handsome, and very hard-working. He carried himself with an air of dignity and pride, and I loved that about him. He took pride in his appearance, and Mama used to say to him, "You stand in front of a mirror like a woman!" Daddy would not allow himself to go gray; he dyed his hair black well into his older years. Verbal and expressive, he told us kids exactly what he expected of us and how he wanted us to behave. He wanted us to be smart and hard-working. At the same time, he was extremely loving and giving. Honest and God-fearing, he taught me how to pray at a young age, and every single night we prayed together on our knees before bedtime.

Faith in God was instilled in us at home, but we couldn't go to church because Daddy worked seven days a week. Sunup to sundown, he drove people back and forth, making good money and also tips. This job, added to the disability payments he received because of his injury at the steel factory, provided our family with a comfortable life.

Every day, Daddy came home for lunch, then returned to work for the rest of the day. I always waited eagerly for him to get home. Dinner was ready by the time he arrived. Mama cooked tasty meals for us, and on weekends and holidays, she

A SILENT FIGHT

made the traditional Southern foods that had been such a big part of my parents' childhoods, such as fried chicken, cornbread, macaroni and cheese, greens, and candied yams. I loved holidays, because that meant my dad would come home after only half a day's work and stay around the house, just relaxing with Mama, all of us kids, and our German shepherd Queenie. Household tasks kept my mother plenty busy, so she didn't have a job outside the home. She cooked delicious meals and cleaned the house daily. We never went hungry. Daddy earned enough to buy our groceries, but he also brought home free food from the grocery store that was getting close to its expiration date.

As a child, I felt especially close to my sister who was just two years older than me. Another sister used to braid my hair sometimes, and even though it felt painful while she was doing it, I was always happy with how it looked when she finished. Along with my siblings and the other kids in the neighborhood, I played outside most of the time if the weather permitted. In those days, parents didn't have to worry about their children's safety as much as they do today. On weekends, we gathered around the TV to watch cartoons and an occasional evening show. Daddy watched the news every single day, and he loved to watch action movies on television.

There were 15-20 houses on our block, and most of them had kids for us to play with. Hide-and-go-seek and freeze tag were fun, but my favorite activity was a made-up game we called "rock teacher." A group of children sat at the bottom of the steps leading up to someone's front porch. Whoever was

A SILENT FIGHT

the "teacher" hid a small rock in their palm and stood in front of them. Each player tried to guess which hand the rock was in, and if they guessed correctly, they got to move up a step. The one who reached the top step first was the winner.

When it came time to start kindergarten, I was so excited and even felt relieved to get out of the house. Being home alone with my mother bored me. She wasn't mean, but neither did she spoil me like my dad did. Besides, all my older siblings were in school, and I wanted to be like them. When the time finally came, I proudly and happily climbed into the car each morning to be driven to school by Daddy, who was protective and preferred to drive us rather than let us walk. I remember doing my schoolwork in the evenings, eagerly spreading my books and papers out on the table because I knew my daddy would tell me how proud he was of me. He loved to sit and watch me write sentences and do math problems. I had a habit of holding my pencil down by the sharpened lead, and that drove him crazy.

"How can you write like that? I can't even see the tip!" he would exclaim.

As a child, I didn't fully understand this but later I realized that Daddy enjoyed seeing me do so well in school because he hadn't had the chance to finish his education when he was young.

"A young me, around 8 or 9 years old, dressed up for picture day-capturing an innocent moment in time."

"A cherished moment with my dad on my birthday-his love and presence made every celebration special."

CHAPTER 2: LIFE ON STANTON STREET

My parents made a big deal out of every single holiday. The food would be ribs, greens, macaroni & cheese, baked beans, corn, potato salad, hamburgers and hot dogs. We had it all. My entire family would gather for the occasion, and the best part of it all, my daddy would come home early, around noon, and would be home all day, doing things like normal people – sitting on the porch, laying around the house, and just taking it easy. I loved to see him home and not working.

Boy, I loved the holidays! I enjoyed watching my neighbors sitting on their porches, welcoming their guests. It made me so happy. My siblings came over to help my mom barbecue. We played music, laughed, joked, just as we did when we were kids.

— Rachel's journal

◊◊◊

As we grew older, Daddy used to say to us, "Take my advice and use only what you need." He emphasized the importance of working hard. "Nothing is free in this world," he said. "And don't call everybody your friend, because not everybody in this world is truly your friend." That was hard advice to absorb at a young age, but later I realized the profound wisdom in it. It's important to know that not

A SILENT FIGHT

everybody has our best interest at heart, and to be careful whom we trust and call our friends.

My parents had a loving relationship, and Daddy spoiled my mother almost as much as he spoiled me. It seemed she felt a little jealous of the attention he paid me, because she used to say, "That's my husband, not yours. When your daddy comes home tonight and we get ready to go upstairs, don't you come up there behind us."

She said that because when I was very small, I would often go into their room at night and he would let me sleep between them in the bed. Mostly Mama tolerated that, but there were some nights when she just didn't want me there!

Daddy provided our mother with everything she needed and a lot of things she wanted. On Sundays, he took us all out driving in his "Sunday car," which he kept for special occasions while using an ordinary vehicle for his work. As we drove along, Mama would sing popular R&B tunes to Daddy. He enjoyed that, and it made us all smile.

We would drive to downtown Detroit and stop at White Castle for hamburgers. I realize now how special that was, because a lot of families around us didn't have enough money to do that kind of thing. We lived like middle-class people, going to restaurants or movies on Sunday, and on weekend trips now and then. Every two years, Daddy drove us to New York or Chicago to stay in a hotel overnight and go shopping. We bought new school clothes, and our mother would shop until she dropped for clothes, jewelry, and purses. Mama also enjoyed shopping in Detroit with money Daddy gave her.

A SILENT FIGHT

When I was little, she took me downtown on a bus with her, and we would spend the day in various department stores.

Daddy loved cars, especially Mercurys, Fords, and Cadillacs that were made right in our city. He always seemed to have a new vehicle. He mostly averaged three cars at a time, but we never had fewer than two because as a jitney, he always needed one available in case one broke down. Whichever happened to be his nicest car was reserved for our Sunday outings, when we would all get dressed up and ready for him to pull in the driveway and pick us up.

Keeping mostly to himself except for a few trusted friends, Daddy had a cautious and protective nature and didn't immediately trust people. He used to say, "I have a PhD in Black people," because through his work as a driver, he witnessed so many things and heard lots of stories. He saw that some people could be mean and cruel, and it gave him trust issues. Because of this, he didn't have many friends; there were only two men that I can remember. I still call Daddy's friend Billy my "godfather" to this day.

Billy was married to Anne, who was the daughter of our neighbor Miss Joyce. They had three children that my sister and I played with, and eventually, after knowing them for years, my father started to allow me and my sister to spend the night at their house. That was the only house I was ever allowed to spend the night at during my entire childhood, and that didn't start until I was about eleven or twelve.

Daddy wanted to know where we were at all times, and insisted we come inside when the streetlights turned on in the evening. But as we grew older, we gained a little more

A SILENT FIGHT

freedom, and life became more about what we children enjoyed doing. Daddy drove us to the roller skating rink on Sundays because we all loved to skate, and he wanted us to do special things. He continued to spoil me, wanting me to be able to buy the things I needed, so he signed for me to have permission to use his Hudson's (now called Macy's) credit card at just 12 years old. When I was 13, still too young to drive legally, he let me drive his nice car around the block two or three times on Sundays when we got home from our family outing.

Daddy paid me $15 to count up his cash at night when he got home from work. He knew I loved math and was good at it. I lined up all the coins and bills, wrote down the total, and rolled it all up with a rubber band when I finished. I felt protective of his money. Daddy kept his tips in a kitchen cabinet, and whenever I caught my mother taking money from his stash, I tattled on her.

We kept a clean house, and on Saturday mornings, my oldest brother, who had the loudest voice in America, would shout, "Get up! Get up!" We all went downstairs and lined up to be assigned our chores. The hardest room to clean was the room where we all ate and watched TV, but as the littlest one in the family, I never had to clean that room. Instead, I was given the easiest chores, like sweeping off the front porch or sweeping down the stairs. After we got our assignments, the same big brother would turn up the volume on the radio or record player, and we all cleaned house together while listening to gospel and R&B tunes.

A SILENT FIGHT

For an hour or so, we would hear, along with the music, the sounds of my sisters working: vacuuming, running water to wash dishes, and running water to clean the bathroom. My siblings made beds, polished coffee tables, and shined mirrors. Once the work was finished, the older kids were free to eat breakfast and go their own way for the day. We younger ones went to the kitchen to get cereal. My second oldest brother raced to the TV to turn it on, and most of the time, we enjoyed watching cartoons before going out to play. However, if certain movies happened to be on TV, we girls were out of luck. My brother loved Star Wars and nothing could get in the way of him watching it. So, my sister and I would watch it with him as he munched on his favorite breakfast sandwich of baloney, ketchup, and black pepper.

On our half-block near the freeway, people sat on their front porches and greeted one another. We all heard the train rumble along the nearby tracks, several times a day. Adults watched out for each other's children and scolded them if they were caught doing something naughty. The neighborhood felt nice and homey, with lots of trees, and because most of our neighbors were homeowners, everyone took good care of their properties.

All in all, Stanton Street in Detroit was a lovely place to grow up.

"My childhood home on Stanton Street-the place where I grew up, creating memories that will last a lifetime."

From my kindergarten graduation to now, Fay has always been by my side. We keep each other close. I am my sister keeper.

"My mom and dad-two incredible souls whose love and guidance shaped my life."

"Celebrating 50 years of love and commitment-my mom and dad at their golden anniversary party."

"My daddy, in his natural element-calm, confident, and full of wisdom."

"Daddy, enjoying a game of basketball in our backyard-forever young at heart."

CHAPTER 3: LOVE FOR A LIFETIME

E*veryone liked my boyfriend, especially my dad. David passed with flying colors with Daddy, which made me not only like him but fall head over heels in love with him.*

— Rachel's journal

◊◊◊

I finally stopped sucking my thumb at age 15 because I had a boyfriend. David Walker had been in elementary school with me, but I'd thought of him as a rough kid and although we were friendly toward each other, I didn't spend much time with him back then. In any case, he wasn't there long, because he moved around a lot.

We reconnected in middle school. David hung out with the popular, partying crowd, and I was just the opposite, not being allowed to go to many places and especially not to parties. But there was no denying our mutual attraction, so we started dating.

Just looking at David gave me butterflies in my stomach. He looked so fine, with his vanilla complexion. He was slightly taller than me, with a build that made heads turn. David was a leader. I can't deny that he was a bit of a bad boy, but he was classy, confident, lovable, and well-loved. I couldn't have asked for anyone better.

David also had an old soul. He'd gotten into quite a bit of trouble because of his tumultuous upbringing, bouncing from place to place. Sometimes he stayed with his mom, but he also often stayed with his aunt, grandparents, or cousin. With little stability, he had too much freedom and that led to trouble. By the time we started dating, he was living with his strict grandmother and becoming more grounded. David valued family and I liked that about him because family was important to me too.

Thankfully, Daddy liked David. That was everything to me! Not that Daddy approved of me having a boyfriend as a teenager, but he chose not to fight it. Instead, he welcomed my boyfriend and was kind to him. He especially liked it when David helped him as he worked on his cars for two or three hours at a time. Through this, they built their own relationship, and it was a solid one.

I wasn't allowed to date on a school night, but on a Friday night, if I got all my chores done, I could go to the drive-in theater with David, or to his grandmother Ivey's house just to hang out. Mrs. Ivey loved me, and I adored her too. David's mother, who lived with Mrs. Ivey off and on, was a street-smart woman, and I learned so much from her. But it was Mrs. Ivey who gave stability to David's life.

When I was 18, my mother found out that David and I had a sexual relationship. When she confronted me about it, I could hardly look her in the face.

A SILENT FIGHT

"You need to tell David that he has to marry you," she said. "If he refuses, then let him go."

I felt so guilty. I was the apple of my dad's eye and now I felt like I was no longer the innocent girl my dad thought I was. How did I let this happen? What was I thinking? What if David broke up with me? How would people look at me?

I told Mama that I would call David, but I felt so nervous to actually do it. I practiced at least 100 times how to say what I had to say. Then, I paged him, and he called me right back. When I told him our choices were to either get married or break up, he said, "Okay." replied.

As soon as he said that my heart sank to the pit of my stomach. I felt certain he wanted to break up.

"Okay what?" I asked.

David shocked me by saying, "Okay, we can get married."

We said "I love you" to each other at the end of our conversation and hung up. I felt so incredibly happy and relieved! Immediately I ran downstairs to tell Mama.

She smiled at me and said, "That's why I like him. I knew he would do the right thing."

I went through the next few days in a daze. *Okay,* I thought, *I do love David, and I do want to marry him, but I can't leave my daddy.* I struggled a bit with that, but nevertheless I made all the arrangements for a civil wedding in Ohio, where we wouldn't have to wait as long to get a license. Daddy agreed to this plan because in my parents' eyes, I was grown up at age 18.

We drove to Ohio, took vows before a justice of the peace, then drove back to Michigan. There was no engagement ring.

A SILENT FIGHT

We had absolutely nothing in the way of possessions, and we had no money. We didn't even have a place to stay! We spent one night sleeping on the floor at my sister's house, and then David went home to his grandmother, and I went home to my parents.

I knew nothing about running a household on my own anyway. Would David even be a good husband? Would I be a good wife? I couldn't predict the future, but I did know that I felt safe with David. I didn't know it then, but he would turn out to be the best husband in the world.

Upon marrying David, I was happy to take his last name, but I still felt I couldn't give up my father's name. So, I hyphenated the two and began going by Rachel Harris-Walker. If I was going to get married and leave my daddy, I could at least honor him by keeping his name.

Through a friend, Daddy found us a vacant two-family flat not too far from him and Mama. David worked in a party store owned by his cousin while I took a job at a local restaurant called Coney Island. It felt weird to have our own place. We had no furniture! When a local furniture store went out of business, it threw some mattresses out on the street. We went out and salvaged two of them, tying them to the top of our car and taking them home. After being cleaned with bleach, they made a perfect bed for us. Looking back, I'm proud of how resourceful we were. We were making the most of an opportunity and living within our means, because we had no money to spare.

Both David and I worked hard to make ends meet. We never had a lot of money, but we also didn't struggle too much

A SILENT FIGHT

because we spent wisely. With few exceptions, we were able to pay all our bills. Once, when we didn't have enough to pay our electric bill and the company threatened to shut off our electricity, David's mother taught me how to negotiate to pay the bill in installments. I was so grateful to learn that!

"A throwback to our teenage years-David and me, before we had children, young and carefree."

David and I on our wedding day-taking our vows for the second time around, a reaffirmation of our love and commitment."

"My mom delivering a heartfelt speech at our wedding, with my dad by her side-two pillars of love and support."

"A precious moment on my wedding day-my dad, about to walk me down the aisle, full of love and pride."

CHAPTER 4: BUILDING OUR FAMILY

The first week was tough. My baby girl had her days and nights mixed up. She slept all day and stayed up all night. David was over every day, staring at her like nothing else mattered in the world. He was in love for sure...

He's here! My handsome little Asian-looking baby boy. His name is David Walker Jr. I love him and I didn't think I could love anything or anyone the way I loved Brittany, but here I am, loving them both exactly the same. I couldn't be any happier. Life is good.

— *Rachel's journal*

◊◊◊

The hardest part about being married was realizing that though we had much in common, we were also different in many ways. It took David and me some time to get used to just letting each other be who we were.

My cooking skills took time to develop. Gradually, I learned to cook for us both. Growing up, I had watched my mother cook, but I'd never done it myself. My meals were simple in the beginning, but eventually, I learned to make more complicated dishes, especially the traditional Southern foods we enjoyed.

A SILENT FIGHT

Not wanting my father to feel like he'd lost his little girl to another man, I visited him and my mother every single day. I was a daddy's girl through and through!

One month after we got married, I started feeling sick and exhausted. After throwing up, I began to suspect I was pregnant, so I quickly ran out and bought a pregnancy test. It was positive! We didn't quite trust the test, so before we made any announcements, we had the results confirmed by a doctor. Again, it was positive.

Becoming pregnant so soon after marrying was a shock for David and me. It scared us a little, but we knew we wanted our baby, and we felt excited to become parents. David already had a son, born when he was just 16. But this time around, he felt more prepared for fatherhood. And I definitely felt excited to become a mother.

Mama was the only one who wasn't surprised about a new pregnancy in the family. It seemed every time she had a dream about fish, one of her daughters would announce a pregnancy. Already, she'd been telling us that one of us must be pregnant, because she'd been dreaming about fish again.

Our beautiful daughter Brittiany Kay Walker was born on February 9, 1990. She was everything to us! I moved back home right before I gave birth because I knew I would need my mother's help. Because I was so young, and this being my first baby, I didn't want to make any mistakes. During that time, David moved back in with his grandmother, and we gave up our first two-family flat. We lived like that for six months, and when I finally felt ready to take care of Brittiany on my own, we moved first to David's grandmother's house.

A SILENT FIGHT

Eventually, we moved into a rental property owned by David's step-grandfather.

A few years after Brittiany's birth, I began to feel the familiar nausea and exhaustion again. This time, I knew I must be pregnant. On April 30, 1993, David Junior, whom we called "DJ," joined our family. He was a beautiful boy! While pregnant with my son, I'd worried that I wouldn't be able to love a second child as much as I loved Brittiany. My fears proved to be unfounded, however, because as soon as DJ appeared, I felt exactly the same intensity of love for him as I felt for my daughter. He was such a joy! We were thrilled to have DJ, and with his arrival, our family felt complete.

I continued to work as a young mother because I was blessed to have my own mom as a babysitter. She watched all my siblings' children too, and we made sure she was compensated for it. I also felt blessed to have a father like David for my children. He was extremely protective, and sometimes that annoyed me, but overall, I felt so lucky to partner with him in parenting.

Mrs. Ivey's husband sometimes took out his anger on her by threatening to throw David, me, and our kids out of the house we rented from him. After he did this one too many times, Mrs. Ivey pushed back. She refused to let him have that power over us any longer. That's when she offered to take out a loan so we could buy our own home. She didn't worry; she knew we could pay the mortgage each month because we worked hard and handled our money well.

At first, it felt nice to be in our own house, but after a while, David wanted to move. From the beginning, he'd had

A SILENT FIGHT

suspicions about the park across the street, and being street-smart, he was right. It ended up being a place where people sat around selling drugs and planning crimes. My husband felt angry as he watched these trifling adults, and fearing his quick temper might get him into trouble, we decided to put the house up for sale as we began searching for a new neighborhood.

The houses that appealed to us all seemed to be too expensive. That discouraged me, because I didn't believe in pipe dreams, or in wanting things that were unreachable, but David knew that if we really put our minds to it, we could make it happen.

David and I wanted more for five-year-old Brittiany and three-year-old DJ than we'd had growing up. In David's youth, he'd spent some time in a group home in the suburbs. While there, he experienced another life than he'd known in the city. A finer life. He had learned that certain things existed and were possible.

Thankfully, everything worked out beautifully! We ended up making a $30,000 profit on our house and back then, that was a lot of money. We took that profit and used most of it to boost our down payment on a house in a diverse and peaceful suburb. We were still very young, and the move was a big step for us, bumping us up into the middle class.

The neighbors welcomed us warmly but they also made sure we knew the rules of the block. We didn't want to disappoint them, so we made every effort to follow those rules. However, we had spent all our money on the move, so we couldn't afford the proper garbage cans all our neighbors used. For a whole year, we put our trash out on the curb in plastic bags, until Mrs. Ivey moved in with us and bought us the right kind of containers.

Since we kept our property looking immaculate, nobody outside our doors knew that we were struggling to keep up financially. Our mortgage was three times the amount of the one on our first house! We were still working at the party store and the restaurant while our neighbors all had higher-paying jobs. Yet, because we were not wasteful people, we managed to always make our monthly mortgage payment.

We felt so grateful to be in a suburb where crime rates were low and, unlike in the city limits, the police responded quickly to any disturbance or emergency call. At last, we felt safe. We heard no gunshots at night. The schools were better, the classrooms smaller. Our neighbors took good care of their properties, even as we did.

Although our neighbors were a bit skeptical of us in the beginning because of how young we were, we lived up to their expectations and became good friends with most of them.

"A timeless moment-my daughter Brittiany, just a newborn bringing endless love and joy to our lives."

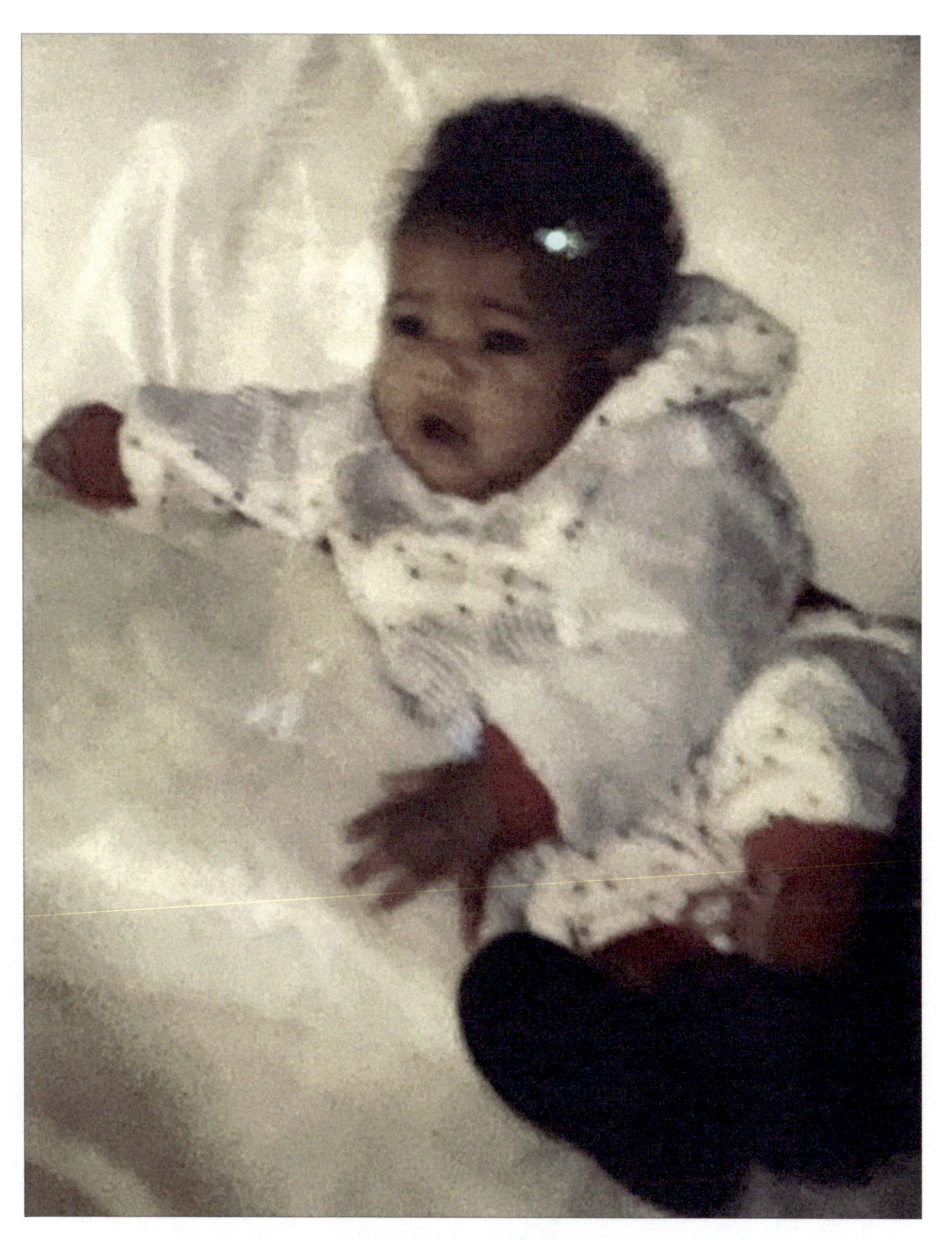

"My son DJ as an infant-small in size but already filling our hearts with so much love."

"Brittiany posing with the Easter Bunny-capturing the joy and magic of childhood."

"DJ meeting the Easter Bunny-another sweet moment filled with childhood wonder."

"One of my favorite pictures–Brittiany and DJ siting side by side. A simple moment that captures how close they are."

"DJ dressed for homecoming, with his big sister/best friend by his side, always supporting him."

"A simple yet cherished family photo with our beloved dog, Bambam. Gone but never forgotten-rest in peace, Bambam."

CHAPTER 5: DREAMS TAKING FLIGHT

A*s years passed by, we went on to great things. Adopted three children, opened a couple of businesses, invested in some real estate, and continued to love and support one another. Through 27 years of marriage, life has been filled with many twists and turns, ups and downs, good and bad, and I have been fortunate to say that life has treated me well and I haven't faced anything that I couldn't handle until now.*
— *Rachel's journal*

◊◊◊

Two years after moving into our house in the suburbs, Mrs. Ivey was still living with us. She had serious health problems, so we had someone come in to take care of her while David and I were working. By this time, I'd left the restaurant and was working in ordering and shipping for a third-party company that functioned as a supplier to Blue Cross.

Each day, during my downtime at work, I made flyers for a daycare business I planned on opening. When Mrs. Ivey passed away, Miss Hatty, her caregiver, stayed on to work for me for a couple of years. The business started small, in my basement, and Hatty took care of the first few customers for

A SILENT FIGHT

me while I continued working. When I got up to five children, I quit my job.

With my own children old enough to be in school by this time, I put my energies into growing the business. I advertised aggressively; soon I was licensed for 12 children and the business just kept expanding. For 12 ½ years, I kept a waiting list. Everyone knew me. They knew we provided great care. I took care of latchkey kids, dropping them off at school in the mornings along with my own children, and picking them up in the afternoons. I dreamed of expanding and opening up a separate facility in the suburbs, but there were few properties for sale in our area.

David advised against renting. He said I couldn't possibly pick up and move my business if a landlord wanted to end a contract. I saw his point but hesitated to buy anything outside of our area because I feared my customers wouldn't follow me to another location. However, when I found a property in Detroit with two buildings side by side, it seemed absolutely perfect. It was already a daycare! I'd gone there to buy used equipment because it was closing down, and instead, we ended up purchasing the whole property.

In 2010, we made the move to the new facility, and to my relief, my customers from the suburbs followed me. We also gained new customers from Detroit. As my Detroit clientele grew, I became licensed for 45 children, and eventually grew to seven employees.

My daycare business is top-notch because caring for people is my calling in life. From my deepest soul, I am a caregiver. Patience is necessary in this career; in fact, I take care of

A SILENT FIGHT

several autistic children. I have never turned down an autistic child, because I believe those children should not be alienated, judged, or sent away simply because they are different. They just require a little more patience and a little more love.

I have some family members working with me, and today, some of the girls I took care of as babies are grown up and working with me too. My daughter Brittiany began helping me at seven years old, handing me diapers when I needed them, helping the children to line up, and taking them to the sink to help them wash their hands. Today, she is the lead infant and toddler teacher at our center.

Back when Miss Hatty took ill and was no longer able to work, I called my mother to ask if she would come and work with me. It took a bit of convincing, but finally, Mama agreed. She stayed for 10 ½ years.

Mama turned out to be a great addition to our team. Getting a paycheck had something to do with that; earning her own money gave Mama a sense of identity and pride. She was able to help my dad pay bills, and she even bought him a car! Mama had always liked to save money. Now, she spent some on herself, but she saved most of it, and she kept encouraging me to save too.

Working with my mother improved my relationship with her. As the youngest child, I'd felt seen by my father, but never by my mother. Now, for the first time, Mama seemed to *see* me as an individual. Daddy was extremely proud of me for starting and growing a successful business. Although Mama never mentioned being proud of me, I knew she approved of what I'd done. Only when Daddy began to have heart health problems did Mama quit working for me. After his triple bypass surgery, my mother stayed home to take care of him and never came back.

My business continued to grow because we loved the children and poured into them as if they were our own. Whenever a new customer enrolled, I told them that I didn't accept just anybody. A potential customer had to be a good fit. I cared about everyone fitting in well and preserving a good atmosphere.

"You are going to see my face every single day," I told the parents. "You'll see me either in the morning or in the evening. I'm here because I care; I love my kids and it's not just about the money. We are raising these kids together."

Not only did some of the children I'd cared for in the beginning come back to work for me, but some of them now bring me their children. Today, I have at least four moms whose diapers I once changed as customers. I am proud to own a business that spans generations.

"A special family photo celebrating my birthday-surrounded by love, laughter and the people who mean the most."

CHAPTER 6: CREATING THE GOOD LIFE

We took our kids skating. We planned trips to Cedar Point, and we didn't go in a car. We got a bus because we knew so many people – my customers, and our friends.

— Rachel's journal

◊◊◊

As it turned out, I was not the only entrepreneur in the family. Upon moving into our new home, David and I realized we had to step up our game in order to keep up with the mortgage payments. That led to David working in the funeral business. He started through a man by the nickname of "Few," a wonderful guy whom David called "Pops." Other people called him "The Body Snatcher." Few picked up bodies and transported them to funeral homes. David started out working for Few, but eventually, he went even further. He bought stretchers and contracted from Few, establishing his own company called "Walker's Removal Service."

Today, we are both still happily running our businesses, and we are still living in our home in the suburbs. The house is paid off. We knew we had to push ourselves to do more to achieve the life we dreamed of, and we rose to the occasion. As we look back over the years, David and I are so proud of what we have achieved, both in our businesses and in our family.

Because David had had too much freedom as a youth and got into trouble because of it, he didn't allow our kids to run freely or spend the night elsewhere. I agreed with him and followed his lead. As a result, we made our house the place all the kids wanted to come and hang out. That way, we could keep an eye on our children and make sure they stayed out of trouble.

As for parenting, David and I were almost always on the same page. Both of us wanted to have close relationships with our children, and both of us wanted an intact, loving family. I made sure to hug and kiss and tell my children I loved them. Because of David's rough start in life, it was important to him that our children feel secure, with both parents actively involved.

I was the chief disciplinarian and David was the talker, but we both believed in the Bible's wise words, *Spare the rod, spoil the child*. Thankfully we didn't have to discipline them too much because they didn't get into trouble very often.

On weekends, after a full week of work, all the cousins would come over. I'd make big pots of spaghetti, chicken, french fries, and other dishes popular with kids. Once their plates were fixed, they would take the food downstairs and hang out. I loved to cook and enjoyed feeding everybody, so we often hosted the holiday gatherings at our home.

David and I took our kids roller skating, just like my father had done for my siblings and me. We also planned trips to Cedar Point on Lake Erie, and because we knew so many

A SILENT FIGHT

people through our business and our kids' school friends, we often rented a 52-seat charter bus for the occasion. We also went to Castaway Bay and a water park in Ohio called Kalahari. And of course, following the example of my own parents, we also chartered a bus and went to New York City to shop for school clothes for the children.

David had a dream of giving back, of helping young people get a good start in this world. He wanted to do this because his grandmother had done it for him. So, we added to our family by adopting three children.

My father had wanted his children to be successful, and we have all done our best to achieve that. As David and I thought about our own children, we knew we wanted the same for them. Success, in our minds, would include getting an education, and that became a goal and a dream of ours as we looked ahead to their futures.

"David and I in our younger years, thrilled to own our first dream car-a Mercedes Benz. A proud and joyful moment."

"Date night with my husband-cherishing every moment together."

CHAPTER 7: THE WILL TO FIGHT

My daddy has always faced health problems, but he has always been a trooper. A self-made, strong man who has always looked sickness in the face and pulled through it like it was nothing. But lately, this sickness seems to be different. It's consistent, and it's not letting up.
— Rachel's journal

◊◊◊

My father was as good a grandfather as he had been a dad. The only problem was that he had so many grandkids that he just didn't have enough time in a day to pay special attention to them all individually. He continued to work long hours, so he didn't see Brittiany and DJ as much as my mother did. Still, they felt they had a close relationship with him. They knew he would come home from work each day with popsicles and ice cream from the grocery store. Although he fussed a little bit now and then, Daddy was a quiet and lovable grandfather the majority of the time.

Over about six years, Daddy experienced health problems. The doctors finally told him that his heart was functioning at only 30%. When he shared this news with me one day when he came to pick up my mother from the daycare, I took it hard. After they left, I went upstairs and unleashed my distress on anything I could get my hands on. I literally tore

A SILENT FIGHT

up my house, knocking things over, smashing objects, throwing things, and overturning tables. I just snapped. My daddy was not well, and I couldn't handle the thought of it.

David tried to talk me through it. He told me that medicine was advanced and that doctors could probably fix my father's heart or at least prolong his life. This calmed me down a little, but I remained generally fearful.

The doctors put a stent in Daddy's heart and stopped the blockage. Three years later he got a pacemaker, and for a time, he seemed to be doing fine. The stent was replaced eventually with no problems, and he went on with his life as usual. Strong and determined, he worked every day. But then his diabetes worsened and began to affect him seriously.

Clearly, Daddy's health was declining. The combination of diabetes, heart problems, and prostate cancer began to take its toll. For the cancer, he had radiation but no chemotherapy. My sister Faye and I rotated taking him to his medical visits and treatments; she took care of all his paperwork, and I scheduled all his appointments. We made a good team.

It was the diabetes that affected Daddy the most. He began to swell from it. Around the same time, it became increasingly clear that he could not keep up with all the repairs in the house he and Mama owned; the place was getting old and had a lot of issues. Our family would often go over to make sure things were in order, shoveling snow, cleaning the kitchen, and straightening up the odds and ends my mother tended to collect. I'd been going there on Sundays even before Daddy got sick, but now we stepped up our visits.

A SILENT FIGHT

For some time already, David and I had been having conversations with my parents about them moving to a new house. Stanton Street was changing, and not for the better. Some of the houses were now abandoned, and one of them had suffered a fire, leaving only a burnt-out shell. The neighborhood didn't feel safe anymore. However, Mama and Daddy refused to leave. There were too many beautiful memories in their home—memories of raising their family and caring for their grandkids. Memories of holidays and other happy occasions. We'd stopped pressing them about leaving, realizing they were going to be stubborn.

But as time went on, it seemed vital to have my parents closer to us. That way, I could make sure they were taken care of and had all they needed. When I brought up the subject of moving again, to my surprise, my parents said they were ready. I was so happy to hear that!

Soon, we began looking for a new house. Around that same time, my next-door neighbor's husband died, and she told me she no longer wanted to live in the house because of the memories. It seemed like an absolute miracle! I begged her to let David and me buy the house from her, and she promised to wait before putting it on the market for a little while so we could try to work out the financing.

We had too much going on credit-wise, so my sister Faye and I worked out a solution in which she would sign for our parents to buy the house next door. We promised Faye that we would have the house paid off in three years. She trusted us to do that. It was equally important to her that my parents move into the house as it was to David and me.

A SILENT FIGHT

Faye signed for the house, but we kept it a secret from our parents while the closing process dragged out, complicated by the fact that David and I had to pay off the seller's liens, water bill, and the cost of repairs on the property.

However, when Daddy was hospitalized for kidney problems associated with his diabetes, Faye, David, and I decided it was time to tell him about the new house. He wasn't doing well at all. It appeared to us that he'd given up, so we thought the news would motivate him to fight to live. We sent DJ to the house, where he put a big red bow on the front door, and then we FaceTimed with him, showing Daddy and Mama the new place.

We made a speech about how great our parents had been over the years, and how they had always been there for us. We wanted them to know they deserved only the best. We handed Daddy a set of keys as he lay in his hospital bed, telling him we had signed for the property and that once we paid off the mortgage in three years, we would give him the title.

Mama started screaming, and Daddy began to cry tears of joy. That was the only time in my life that I ever saw my father cry. Just as we'd hoped, the thought of moving into a new home right next door to us revived his spirits.

"This has given me the will to fight," he said.

"This photo brings back so many memories-every lesson, every laugh ,every bit of love. Daddy, you are with me always."

CHAPTER 8. LOSING DADDY

My dad meant the world to me and anyone close to me knew it. Doctor's appointment after doctor's appointment, we felt we had it all under control. Everything seemed to be fine until I got a call from Faye saying that one of Dad's doctor's appointments didn't go so well. She was about to take him straight to emergency because they were concerned about his blood pressure. Instantly my heart dropped to the pit of my stomach. Immediately I began praying, asking God to let my dad be okay.

— Rachel's journal

◊◊◊

Sure enough, Daddy got some of his strength back. It felt just perfect, having my parents next door. I was there every day, babying and waiting on my daddy. Our relationship was unique. Daddy had a way of playing sick whenever he saw me coming, even when he wasn't feeling bad. He'd been doing that for years because he loved the attention I gave him. Everyone seemed to catch onto it but me, and when I finally did, it warmed my heart. In return, I spoiled him even more.

My dad meant the world to me and anyone close to me knew it. Faye and I were taking care of him, making sure he got to all his doctor's appointments, and I began to feel like everything was under control. But around eight months after

A SILENT FIGHT

my parents moved next door, I got a call from Faye saying that one of Dad's medical appointments didn't go so well. She told me she was getting ready to take him straight to the emergency room because of concerns about his blood pressure.

Instantly my heart dropped to the pit of my stomach. I began praying, asking God to let my dad be okay. He went into the hospital to get his blood pressure under control, and as they worked with him from day to day, I was sure to be there as much as possible. Those daily visits helped me get through it.

As he lay in his hospital bed, my dad was talking to us like usual and seemed to be doing okay. On Friday, the 13th of May, I called him and told him that David and I were planning to go out of town for the weekend to celebrate our wedding anniversary on the 15th, but that we would come to see him before we left.

Daddy encouraged us to go and have fun. "Don't be like me," he said. "Don't just work all the time. Go and live your life."

As we were on our way to the hospital with Mama in the car, my phone rang. A nurse told me that my father had just gone into cardiac arrest. I felt numb, almost as if my soul had left my body. "I'll be there in less than five minutes," I said into the phone.

As soon as we pulled up to the hospital, I jumped out of the car and ran as fast as I could up to his room. A nurse met me at the door and asked if I wanted them to continue doing CPR. I said yes. How could they possibly think I wouldn't want that? As I stood outside the door, I could hear the doctors and nurses working on him. I felt traumatized. Screaming, I fell to the floor.

Never will I forget a male nurse I encountered on that terrible day. As I collapsed onto the floor, he came and held me, talking me through it. He calmed me down, speaking to me in a caring and kind voice. Another nurse seemed hardened and insensitive, as if she had been doing her job for far too long. A few days after my father's cardiac arrest, she came into his room with a little black box to perform a procedure, sticking him with needles to see whether he was responsive or had brain damage. Her manner was almost robotic as she went about her task.

I couldn't receive anything this particular nurse said because of how blunt she was. She remained straight-faced, showing no emotion. I didn't like her. After encountering her, I knew I could not leave the hospital and abandon my father to someone who didn't care about him. That's when I made arrangements to move into the hospital.

I'd chosen Bloomfield Hospital for my father because it was smaller, and I believed that its location in a majority-white suburb would mean better care for him. I hadn't wanted him at Henry Ford Hospital in the city because I'd heard stories of substandard care there. Yet at Bloomfield, I felt at times that the staff was not truly paying attention to my father.

Bloomfield had a room that I could spend the nights in as long as I called to reserve it by a certain time each morning. I moved my things in and made sure to make that call every day. David moved in with me. Our children were old enough

A SILENT FIGHT

to be alone by then, so all David had to do was check in with them each day. Brittiany ran the daycare for me while I was gone, along with my skilled and supportive staff.

I stayed with Daddy all day, and at night, after a full day of work, DJ would come in to take over. In my constant worry and sadness, I somehow failed to notice how hard this was on my son. For two months, he worked all day long and then came to sit with his grandpa all night. At that point, the doctors told us they had done all they could do at Bloomfield and that my father needed to move to another facility.

If they told me I could take care of my father at home, I knew I would be ready and willing to do that. But they said his care was too complicated for that. They suggested a rehab center in Ohio, but I wasn't okay with him going so far away. He wasn't responsive, but I still wanted to visit him daily and for him to sense my presence somehow. They found a place for him at a facility called St. John's. It wasn't far from where I lived, but its staff wouldn't let me spend the nights there and were very strict about visiting hours.

On July 13, 2016, the staff at St. Johns informed us they were going to transport Daddy back to Bloomfield for tests. Somehow, I knew in my heart that he didn't have long to live. Brittiany went to St John's in my place because my heart was heavy, and I didn't feel I had the strength to do it. From there, she rode with Daddy in the ambulance to Bloomfield.

Along the way, Daddy went into cardiac arrest and passed away with Brittiany by his side. She witnessed him taking his last breath. David and I rushed to Bloomfield only to learn the terrible news that my beloved father was gone.

A SILENT FIGHT

Although his death wasn't a surprise to any of us, my whole family —my mother, children, nieces, nephews, siblings, husband, and myself —took it extremely hard. Daddy was so loved by us all.

Celebrating the Life of

Frank Leandro Harris

July 22, 1938   July 13, 2016

Saturday, July 23, 2016
Family Hour 10:00am   Funeral Service 11:00am

Mt. Calvary Baptist Church
1720 East State Fair
Detroit, MI 48203

House Minister Officiating

"My dad's life, his legacy, his impact. We made sure he was honored like the king he was. He deserved nothing less."

A tribute to my father–a golden chain that carries his memory, and reminds us of how much he meant everything to us.

CHAPTER 9. FIGHTING THE DARKNESS

When I was going through my depression, it was always as if it was dark around me. I knew it was summer; I could feel the heat but it never looked like a summery day to me. It looked dark and sad. I would be driving down the street from work, and I could look to the left of me and see cars and people playing their music and being happy, and I didn't understand that.

—Rachel's journal

◊◊◊

In the aftermath of my father's passing, I was too grief-stricken to realize that my children had also been traumatized by losing him. My son had lost sleep, spending every night in the hospital at Daddy's bedside, watching him gradually slip away. Brittiany had been with him when he died. I had absorbed the pain of his loss without comprehending how painful it was for my children too. Later, their pain would come out in various ways. My son started drinking. My daughter grew depressed and had crying spells.

Not only were my children hurting from losing their granddad, but they were hurting because they could see that something was terribly wrong with me. I had warned David that if anything ever happened to my father, I would need everybody to rally around me to help me get through it. But in truth, I didn't let people get close enough to help.

For one thing, I hardly came out of my bedroom. Later I switched to lying in the back room of our house, but regardless of where I chose to spend my time, the result was the same: I kept myself isolated and buried under a mountain of grief. When I did talk to my concerned family members, I spoke of wanting to die, of having no reason to live anymore. This frightened and upset them, but I was too absorbed in my own pain to even notice that.

My son DJ would come into my room and beg me to choose life. "I can't live without you," he said. Thinking it would give me a reason to stay on this earth, DJ even purposely fathered a child with his girlfriend. At the time, I understood his motives and it did help some, but I had little patience with my family's constant expressions of concern. I felt like everyone else was being selfish and insensitive to what I was going through.

The cycle continued: my loved ones worried about me, but in my anger, I pushed them away, wanting to be alone.

In the beginning, David tried to take a stern approach toward me. "You're going to be okay," he insisted. "Are you going to just lay here all day again? You can't just lay here; you've got to get up!"

Rather than helping me, his scoldings only made things worse. My husband desperately wanted me to be strong. He meant well, but I just could not process my grief the way he

A SILENT FIGHT

wanted me to. Thankfully, David never left my side; he stuck by me despite my inability to "snap out of it."

David also introduced me to a comedy show on TV at that time, and that distracted me for a while. He and my children could laugh and be silly and enjoy funny things, whereas I had always had a more serious personality. Now, I desperately needed to laugh. I used to ask him to turn on the show, because it kept me occupied and took my mind off the pain, if only temporarily.

When my little grandson was around, I put on music and danced with him in the kitchen, knowing I had to make an effort for his sake. My granddaughter came over frequently and that helped too.

Of course, Mama also took Daddy's death very hard. There were days when she would scream so loud the neighbors could hear her. Not only did I have to carry my grief, but I shouldered hers too. I mostly spoke to her from her front porch, because I couldn't bear to go into the house where Daddy had spent the last eight months of his life.

During those dark days of depression, catching a whiff of crisp, fresh air or seeing an old car took me immediately back to my childhood on Stanton Street. I felt lost in the past whenever that happened. Not wanting to think about those happier days, I tried to put the memories out of my mind but was seldom able to. Instead, I would start crying and feel like I wanted to die.

Years passed. I managed to get up in the mornings and drag myself to work. Being around the children in my daycare always cheered me up, and I tried never to be sad around

A SILENT FIGHT

them. For nine hours out of each day, I escaped my depression. But as soon as I came home from work, I slipped back into the darkness, burying myself under the covers, struggling to find the will to live.

Within the first eight months after Daddy's death, I got a tattoo of his face on my arm. I'd had to wait months for that appointment, but having something to look forward to give me a reason to keep going. Because I struggled with suicidal thoughts, I hoped that looking at an image of my father every day might help me, and I told the tattoo artist that he was probably saving my life. It helped for a while, but ultimately, it wasn't enough to keep me from sinking into depression. I also wore a special necklace with a picture of my father. I couldn't go anywhere without it. If I happened to forget it, David would immediately bring it to me at work, knowing I couldn't function without it.

Various obsessions and addictions came next. Trying to do whatever I could to get me through the day, I began to shop like crazy, running up debt on my credit cards. I even bought a new car. After a month, depression settled over me again.

Looking back, I don't believe I was being selfish on purpose. I simply didn't know how to move forward. As their concern deepened, my family could do nothing but watch and wait.

For about six years, I barely scraped by, pretending to live a normal life. I'd learned to cope and to function, but I still hadn't recovered my joy of living. My family could see I was merely getting by, going through the motions, still lost in depression.

A SILENT FIGHT

One day I pulled my car into our driveway and could not summon the strength to get out and walk into my house. I had put a suicide hotline number into my phone, and I decided right there and then to call the number. But before I could do so, Brittiany pulled up behind me. That caused me to plummet deeper into depression. Could I really live one more day without getting help?

My family tried so hard to help me, but they could not help me the way I needed to be helped. They desperately wanted me to live when all I wanted to do was die. I sensed that if I could just talk to someone with experience, maybe there would be some answers; maybe they could help me out of the depths of my darkness.

Suicidal thoughts persisted for what seemed a very long time. I owned a licensed gun but thank God I didn't really know how to work it. I thought about taking pills or cutting my wrists. But Brittiany kept reminding me that I had supported her throughout her pregnancy by telling her she could do it, and that she would be a great mother.

"You encouraged me as I brought Skyler into the world," she said, "and now you want to leave me here to raise her without you?"

My son had also had a child just for me. Could I toss aside such a beautiful gesture on his part?

I didn't want to live, but I couldn't actively choose death.

The depression played tricks on my mind. I had a hard time organizing my thoughts and became increasingly forgetful. A couple of times, I paid my employees twice because I couldn't remember that I had already made

A SILENT FIGHT

payroll. Thankfully, they were honest and told me I had already paid them. I paid my car note multiple times. I got into car accidents, crashing into other cars because I was in a daze. When I felt depression coming on, I would rub my thumbs and fingers together and begin tapping my feet—nervous gestures that made me feel like I was getting ready to fight off the darkness. Whatever happened, I could not let it take me all the way down, because that's when suicidal thoughts would come.

Then, came a turning point at last.

"Introducing our little blessing, Skyler. From the beginning, she's been pure love and joy." 2/4/2015

"Skyler growing more beautiful every day. Watching her change and blossom is pure joy."

" Introducing my grandson, Bryson. From the moment he arrived, our hearts have been full." 7/19/2020

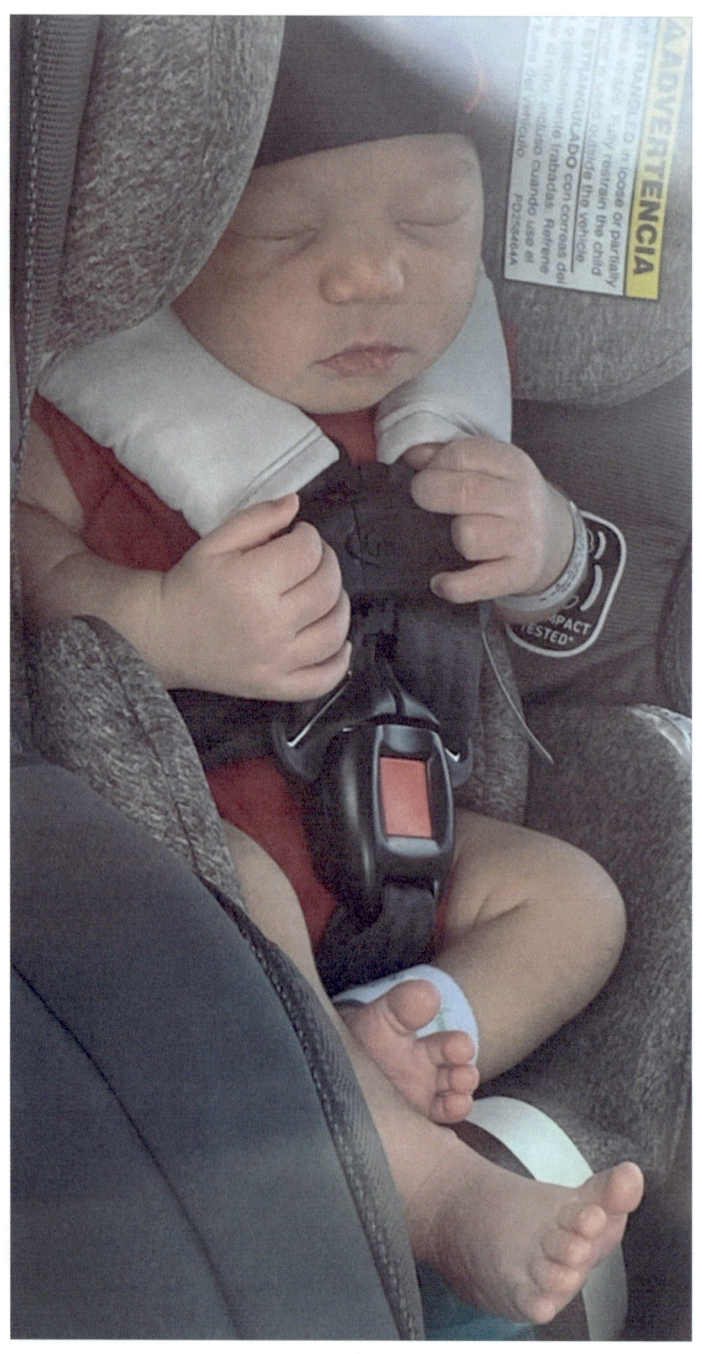

"The day he came home, our hearts were forever full. Our little one, a blessing from the very start."

CHAPTER 10. FINDING THE LIGHT

I started listening and started trying. They'd say, "Granddaddy would be proud of you if you'd just go on to work and be strong and do the things you were doing before." I finally started hearing that. I'd always wanted to make my daddy proud. So, I started pushing through . . .

◊◊◊

One night, while sleeping, I felt myself leaving my body, rising from the bed, and walking past my dresser toward the door of my room. Suddenly, I saw my father standing there. Overjoyed, I ran to him, shouting, "Daddy!"

He looked at me with a stern expression. "Go back!" he commanded.

"What?" I cried. "I'm not going back! I want to be with you."

I felt comfortable with dying, with no longer going through the motions of living. My children could get by without me, and I longed for relief from the pain, darkness, and sadness.

But my father would not be persuaded. He yelled at me in a loud and angry voice, "Go back now!"

Daddy had never spoken to me like that before. Only rarely, during my childhood, had I heard him use that tone with my mother. His tough, angry demeanor left me stunned and bewildered. I wanted to be with him so badly! A light seemed

A SILENT FIGHT

to emanate from him, and I just knew I wanted to be in that light. Gazing at him, I no longer felt any pain. How could he not let me stay with him?

I knew I had to obey him. I turned around and walked back the way I had come, and I felt my body fall into the bed.

That's when I woke up.

What happened that night did not feel like a dream to me. There is such a thing as "broken heart syndrome," also known as "stress cardiomyopathy." It is brought on by extreme stress and can be fatal in rare cases. I have always believed that I died that night, and no one can convince me otherwise.

The encounter with my father enabled me to begin climbing out of the deep hole I had been living in for so long. After that night, I stopped trying to die. I stopped wanting to die because I felt that wasn't what my daddy wanted me to do, and I wanted to respect his wishes. So, I started to try.

I began to listen to my husband and children. Before, when they said things like, "You've got to try harder," or "Grandaddy wouldn't want to see you like this," I'd brushed them off, refusing to hear them. Now, for the first time in a long time, I made an effort to actually hear what they were saying.

I went out and bought myself some wall plaques with positive sayings on them, like "Smile," and "Today will be a good day." Each morning, I would look at those and psych myself up to face another day. David and I went so far as to remodel our home, installing white marble floors to help

A SILENT FIGHT

combat the darkness I struggled with whenever depression came on.

Gradually, things started to get a little easier.

I did not seek out counseling, although now I wish I had. I did not share the story of my encounter with friends because I feared they wouldn't understand, but I did share it with David, my children, my sister Faye, and my niece Tiffany and her husband Marques. Marques gave the best hugs, and words weren't needed because those comforting hugs showed me how much he cared.

As I began to make an effort, David encouraged me by telling me how proud he was of me.

Yet I still felt raw and vulnerable. If David, a music lover, put on old R&B tunes, I was reminded of my father and quickly spiraled downward again. When I washed dishes and the window blinds above the sink were open, I caught a glimpse of my father's green Ford Explorer in the driveway next door and once again felt the desperate pain of missing him. I learned to keep the blinds closed, and I asked David to be very careful about what kind of music he played.

If David and I were driving in the car and the radio was on, I could sink into depression when a certain old tune came on. Even if David quickly switched it off, it was too late. At that point, I was ruined for wherever we were going. To prevent this from happening, my husband and I began driving to events in separate cars.

Once, at a wedding, a song was played that made me cry. Desperately I searched for the nearest exit, not wanting to spoil the happy occasion for other people.

A SILENT FIGHT

Whenever I lost it over such reminders of my father, my family would worry all over again because they could see I had not healed. They started to tiptoe around as if walking on eggshells, keeping the blinds closed, keeping the radio off. But it was almost impossible for them to prevent me from being triggered.

Still, I made baby steps forward. With my family's love and support, I eventually came to a place of healing. It's an ongoing process, but today, I can honestly say that I have recovered my joy of living, one day at a time. I know for certain that my struggle is not over, but I have gained the strength and the will to fight. Now I understand the terminology, "It's okay not to be okay." I have indeed come to a place of being okay with not being okay, fully understanding that I am living with a broken heart and will die with one.

"A moment of strength, wearing black but finding the light, fighting my way out of the darkness, one step at a time."

A memorable moment of my husband and I, celebrating our Anniversary. Each moment together is a celebration of our love.

"This is my beautiful daughter—the one who held me together through my darkest day. I love her more than words can say."

"My son-the one who could see when I was hurting. He stood right by my side. His love and strength meant everything."

"My grandchildren-my greatest blessings, my deepest love and the inspiration behind my healing journey".

"The Walker's-A family built on love, strength, and support for one another. Unbreakable family ties." #FamilyForLife

CHAPTER 11. REACH FOR THE SUNSHINE

So, I went through a lot of hard stages. If I had gotten counseling, I would have healed sooner. This is what I want people to do. Get the help! I was self-helping, like self-medicating, and it was hard. I don't think it would have taken me so long to get to the place I am now if I had reached out for help sooner . . .

◇◇◇

Today, my son and daughter are doing much better. When I started to heal, the whole family started to heal. I adore my granddaughter Skyler and my grandson Bryson, who just happens to look and act like my father. He even has my dad's complexion.

Reader, if you have lost someone dear to you, follow my advice and try to grieve in a healthy way from the very beginning of your loss. You have to start out fighting. You must fight not to even slip down into depression, because depression is the hardest fight. Try not to go there. I allowed myself to sit in depression for far too long, and I can testify that it is the darkest place imaginable. It's dark, and it hurts. The sun is shining outside, but you don't see it.

A SILENT FIGHT

Avoid avoiding people. Don't say to those who care about you, "I don't want to talk," or "Call me back another time." Do not hide from the people who are rallying around you. Because I didn't want to hear people reminding me that my father was gone, I kept to myself and tried to block them out. I didn't want to think about it, but that's what dragged me down.

Allow people in, and don't avoid talking about your loss. The more you talk, the more you can heal. Depression sets in when you stop talking. Hiding made me worse. If you don't hide; if you face it head on, you can allow yourself to start healing.

Believe me, I know the temptation of checking out. When you're in pain, you want the pain to go away, and the pain disappears when you sleep. When you shut the door of your room and it's just you, you're going to feel some pain, but it seems better than the pain you feel when you open the door to the world and hear everyone talking about your loss. Even worse, you see people walking around, living their lives as if nothing happened. That's where the anger comes in.

Really? They want me to act normal? How can they laugh and joke and move on with their lives when I'm hurting so badly?

You might think if you stay in your room you won't have to see all that. But if you stay in that room with the door shut, depression will carry you away to a dark place that is hard to come out of.

I strongly urge you to confront your pain and talk about it. Do this from the very beginning! That's what therapists are

A SILENT FIGHT

for, and you should see one immediately. I wish I had. Or at least listen to the people around you who love you and allow them to help you. I refused to let my loved ones help me. Don't be like me! Please, PLEASE reach out for help! If you are deep in depression and feeling suicidal, I plead with you to call the numbers listed at the end of this chapter.

I was afraid to see a therapist because I knew they would talk about my loss, and I wanted to avoid talking about it. Now, looking back, I realize I desperately needed to have that conversation. Talking is how you heal. I also needed to open up my blinds and see my father's car sitting there, so that reality could sink in. Stubbornly refusing to do so postponed my healing. In that process, I was hurting myself and hurting everybody around me who loved me and cared about me.

If I had only talked with my family, I would have known that my son and daughter were hurting, and we all could have sought out help. But of course, I didn't do that.

I could not continue to heal from this journey of grief if it wasn't for God and me knowing his Word and his promises. My father was a God-fearing man. Daddy always said, "When someone dies, we should not cry for them; we should be joyful." I held onto that.

As I lay in my dark room, I knew that God was real, and that I was not supposed to question him. I never did. Although I was hurt by the loss of my father, I didn't blame God for it. I just prayed for him to help me get better. I heard my grown son begging me to live, but I couldn't come out of my depression on my own. So, I asked God to fix my mind.

A SILENT FIGHT

Even in my depressed state, I knew something was not right with me and that I needed healing.

Today, to maintain my progress, I pray a lot, and I stay positive. My experience in the depths of depression has given me much more compassion for people who have mental health challenges, who live on the streets because they cannot function anymore in a normal capacity. I was so very close to that myself. I nearly lost i! This world meant nothing to me, and I didn't want to live in it any longer. I forgot my purpose in life.

I now understand how fragile we are, and that we can be broken. There are people out there who lose a loved one in a violent way. My father at least left this world peacefully. I had months to be by his side, watching over him, telling him I loved him. Because I know there are people in this world who lose loved ones suddenly and violently, I have learned to be thankful for the way my father passed.

These days, I am able to remember happy things about my father, and even laugh at certain memories. I'm doing so much better. I have opened the blinds. Knowing Daddy would approve, I have been able to let go of two of his cars and give them to my brothers, and I am even in the process of repairing my father's Ford Explorer so I can start driving it. My kids and husband see that as real progress and are so excited. It's a sign to them and to everyone who knows me of how well I am doing. Driving his car is my special way of remembering him. Like Daddy, I love cars, especially high-end foreign brands like Range Rovers and Mercedes. And just like Daddy, I kept three cars at a time for many years. This year, I

A SILENT FIGHT

finally realized I don't need three cars, so I am letting go of my "hobby."

Mama lives with us now. Both of us are finally over the hump. Grief brought on dementia in my mother; she didn't eat, lost weight, and began to forget things. She is much more comfortable living with David and me. Once she moved in, I started to see her condition improve.

Lately, I'm pushing myself toward being able to listen to the old tunes we used to play as a family, the classic R&B tunes Mama sang to Daddy on those long-ago Sunday drives. Maybe one day soon I'll feel strong enough to look at old family photographs. Little by little, I'm moving toward that milestone.

I am still broken, but I am living with a broken heart whereas before, I wanted to die with a broken heart.

We don't know how strong we are until we are faced with serious challenges. I didn't think I would be strong enough to write this book, but here I am.

I believe that God has given each of us our own life to live, and although other people come into our lives, we can't just give up on life when it's time for them to leave. Because God gave me this life, I am determined to keep moving forward, no matter how hard it might be.

**Suicide and Crisis Lifeline:
988
Languages: English and Spanish
Available 24 hours**

A SILENT FIGHT

**National Suicide Prevention Lifeline
1-800-273-TALK (8255)**

This tattoo, a symbol of strength and survival. It gave me the courage to fight when I was lost and severely depressed.

"Here I am- at the end of my book, proud of every chapter."

"Holding the weight of both struggle and strength. Suicide and resilience-two sides of my journey, but resilience wins."

RACHEL HARRIS-WALKER

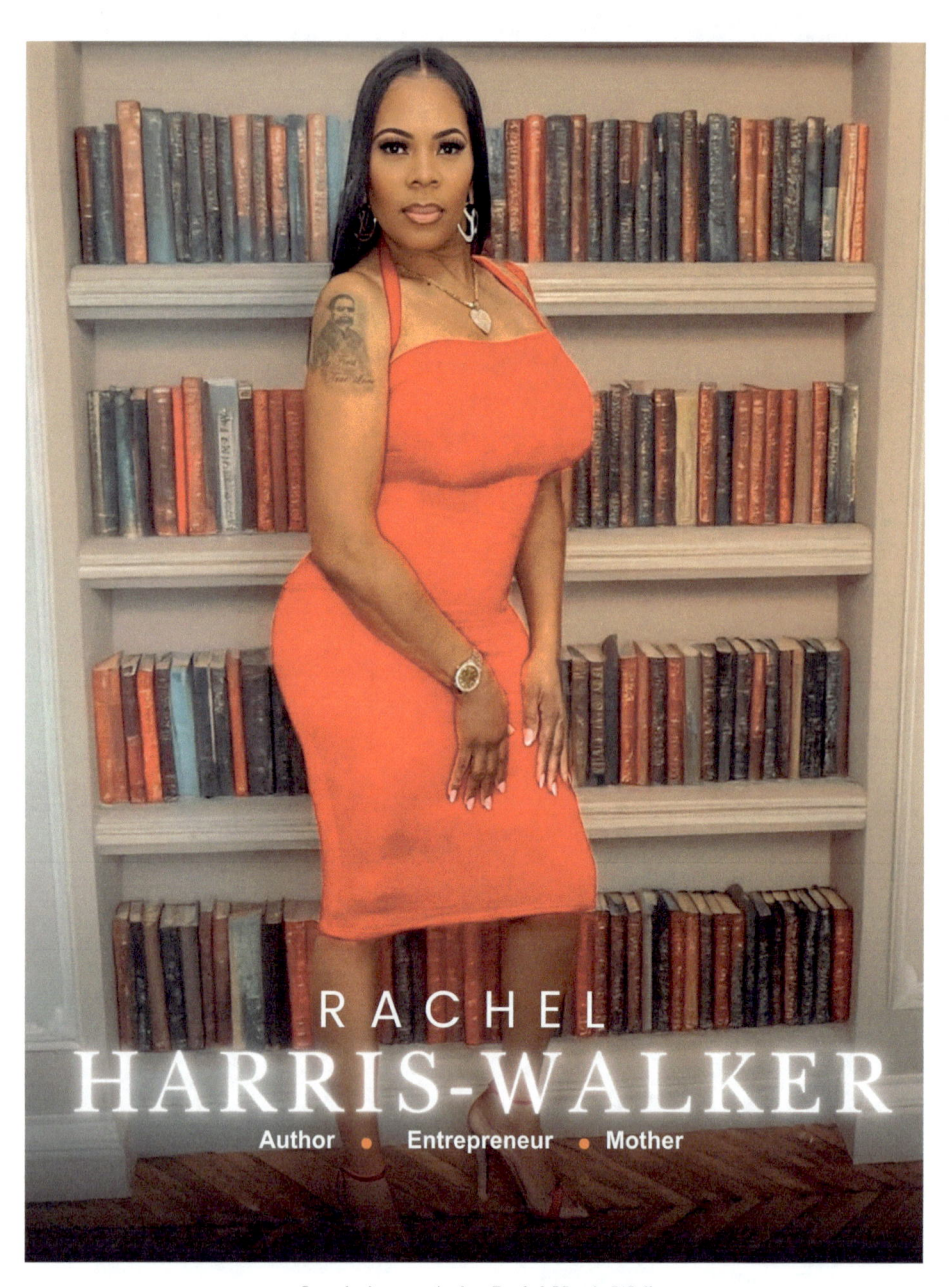

Author • Entrepreneur • Mother

Introducing...... Author Rachel Harris Walker

ACKNOWLEDGEMENTS

First, I want to thank my husband for standing by my side from the start of my dad's illness and through my darkest moments. You cared for him, took him to appointments, and supported me through my depression. Your unwavering love and strength helped me pull through.

To my daughter Brittiany, thank you for being my rock. You stepped in to manage things when I couldn't, and you were there with my dad during his final moments. Watching him pass was incredibly difficult, and I could never repay you for your strength and love during that time. Please know how much I deeply appreciate you. Your support and love mean the world to me.

To my son David (DJ), thank you for always being there to listen and comfort me. You showed up when I needed you most, offering steady love and support throughout it all. You constantly reminded me to fight, to keep going, and that I wasn't alone. Your encouragement was a lifeline during my darkest days.

To my grandchildren, Skyler and Bryson, you are my heart and my inspiration. Skyler, as the oldest, and Bryson, as the youngest, you are my main reasons for fighting. Your love, laughter, and light remind me every day why life is worth living. I love you both more than words can express.

To my sister Faye, thank you for your understanding, patience, and unconditional care. You supported me with so much love, and I am forever grateful.

To my bonus daughters, Tamira and Kalista, thank you for helping me through my sad days with your love and kindness. Most importantly, thank you for stepping in to help care for my mom during such a difficult time. Your support meant everything to me, and I will always be grateful.

To my niece Tiffany, thank you for your kind words and encouragement that helped me through tough days.

And to Marques, thank you for your warm hugs that always made me feel safe, loved, and comforted.

Lastly, I want t thank Family Foods Superstore and its owner Jimmy for continuing to honor my dad. From the time of his passing to today, his obituary has remained posted at the front of your office. This act of love and respect speaks volumes about the bond you shared with him, and it means so much to me and my family.

Thank you all for being my light in the darkest times.

"The most treasured photo of my dad–so vivid, so full of memories. A priceless reminder of loving moments we shared."

ABOUT THE AUTHOR

Rachel is a devoted wife, a loving mother, and a compassionate daughter. A woman of faith with a strong entrepreneurial spirit, she has spent over 25 years running a successful daycare, dedicating her life to nurturing and uplifting others. Passionate about her community, she is both a generous giver and a dedicated advocate, always striving to make a meaningful impact. As a bold and confident Aries, she embraces leadership with strength and determination. Now, she embarks on a new journey as an inspiring author, sharing her powerful story with the world.

Made in the USA
Columbia, SC
20 April 2025